T5-AOI-542

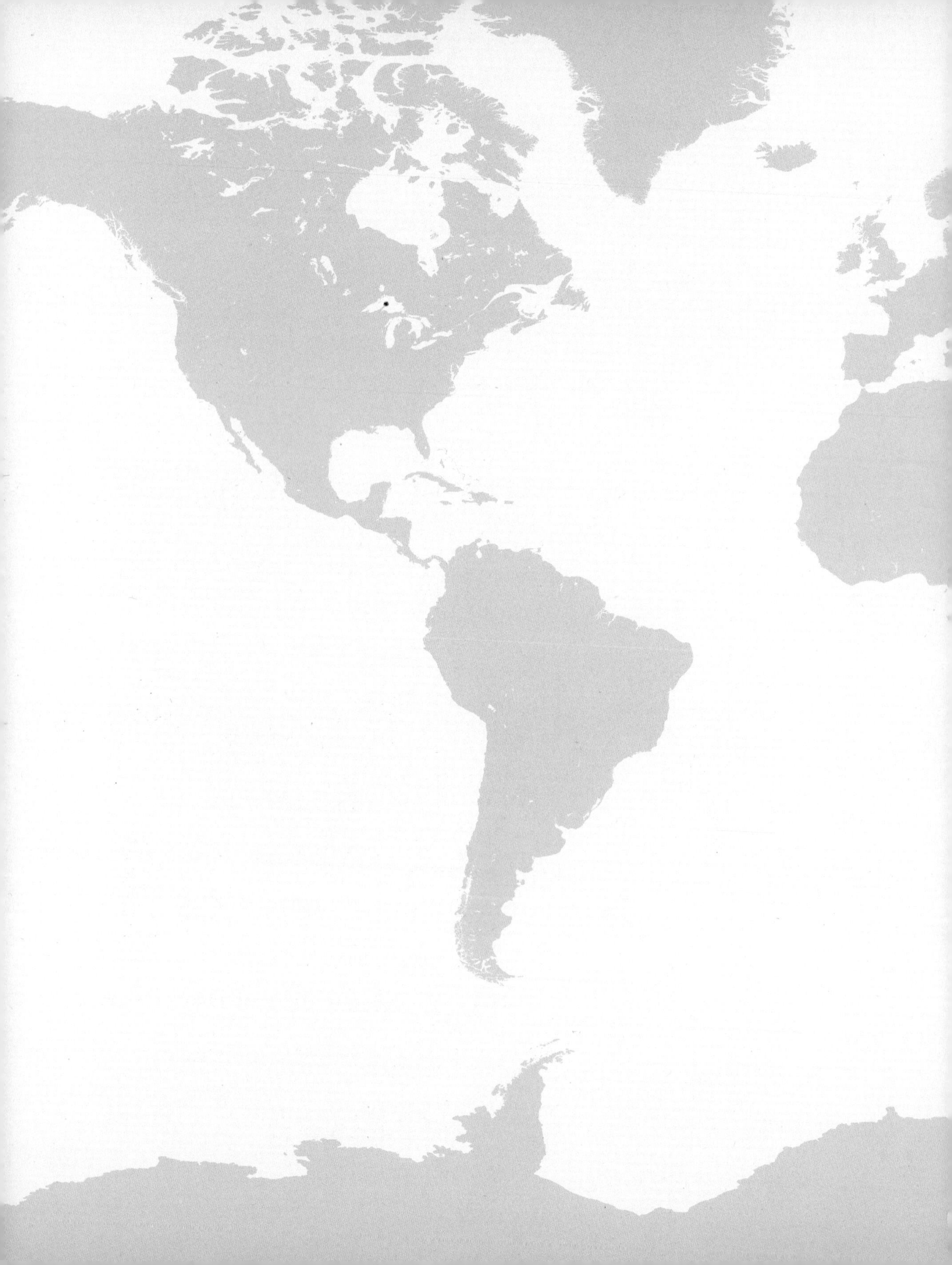

AROUND THE WORLD

Letters from Children
Across the Nations

STEFANIE BOYLES

ARCTIC OCEAN

NORTH
AMERICA

United
Kingdom

France

Morocco

PACIFIC OCEAN

Peru

SOUTH
AMERICA

SOUTH
ATLANTIC
OCEAN

EUROPE

Russia

ASIA

Mongolia

Turkey

Japan

PACIFIC OCEAN

Egypt

Saudi Arabia

North Korea

AFRICA

Bangladesh

Afghanistan

Cambodia

Indonesia

INDIAN OCEAN

AUSTRALIA (OCEANIA)

SOUTHERN OCEAN

ANTARCTICA

INTRODUCTION

Jesus's last words to His disciples are familiar to many of us. We call it *the Great Commission*, and it is found in Matthew 28:18-20:

> Jesus came near and said to them, "All authority has been given to me in heaven and on earth. Go, therefore, and make disciples of all nations, baptizing them in the name of the Father and of the Son and of the Holy Spirit, teaching them to observe everything I have commanded you. And remember, I am with you always, to the end of the age."

Last words should be embraced as lasting words. The command to continue God's global mission is just as relevant today as it was to the disciples. The Great Commission is for *every single one of us*. As disciples of Christ, we should be sharing the gospel and discipling others. We do this in the context of our homes, workplaces, and neighborhoods. However, we should not forget to consider those outside our local vicinities. There are billions of underserved, unreached, and unengaged people groups across the world.

The Heart of This Resource

God's mission has always been a global mission (Genesis 12). We want to be strategic in how we cultivate a global outlook for our children. The heart behind this resource is to *equip* you to do this. It is to *inform* parents and children alike that there are many people around this world today who have never heard the good news of Jesus Christ. It is a way to *invite* families to pray for these unreached people groups and pray for those serving them, now and in the future.

Prayer is a tremendous way we can join God in His global mission. And just maybe, the conversations that follow may be seeds planted in our children's hearts to be missionaries when they are older.

May we allow these stories to make us a bit uncomfortable. May they be springboards for discussions in our homes about the realities of this fallen world. And ultimately, may we remind each other that Jesus is "the way, the truth, and the life" (John 14:6). Despite the brokenness, sin, and needs of this world, each and every one of us finds redemption, healing, and restoration in the person and work of Christ alone.

> **SHARING THIS GOSPEL TRUTH — IN WORD AND DEED — IS THE MOST LOVING THING WE CAN DO FOR OTHERS, NEAR AND FAR.**

TERMS & TOPICS
FOR DISCUSSION

UNREACHED PEOPLE GROUPS

People groups considered "unreached" are groups in which the community itself lacks adequate numbers of believers and resources to evangelize the group. There could be a small percentage of believers, but these believers would benefit from outside assistance to effectively share the gospel with the entire people group.

FRONTIER PEOPLE GROUPS (FPGS)

People groups that fall into this category have less than or equal to 0.1% Christians. This means that there is no gospel-movement within this group that is considered sustainable. There are over 1.5 billion people in the world today who fall into various FPGs. These people have almost no chance of hearing the good news of Jesus unless someone from outside their people group comes to share the gospel with them.

10/40 WINDOW

This window is a rectangular area on the world map between 10 degrees north and 40 degrees north latitude. These coordinates cover North Africa, the Middle East, and Asia. The countries that fall within this area are considered the most unevangelized. The majority of Muslims, Hindus, and Buddhists also reside within this area. There are approximately 5 billion people who live within the window, and over half of them are considered unreached.

PIONEER WORKERS

Pioneer workers are people who engage in church planting efforts within unreached people groups. Some organizations will calculate how many pioneer workers are needed in each country. Often, the ratio they use is 1 worker for every 50,000 persons.

ISLAM

Islam is the second-largest religion in the world. People who practice Islam are called Muslims. There are at least 1.5 billion Muslims in the world. They believe there is one god named Allah.

HINDUISM

Hinduism is a major world religion, and it began in India. It is a religion that believes in the existence of many gods, but they believe that one supreme god lives in each person's soul. Hindus believe in things like reincarnation (people's souls coming back as someone or something else after death) and karma (the sum of a person's deeds throughout a lifetime). There are approximately 1.2 billion Hindus in the world.

BUDDHISM

Buddhism is another religion that originated in India. Some people consider it a philosophy. It is considered the path to enlightenment and requires people to look to meditation and morality to embrace truth. They believe that a person will receive wisdom if his or her mind is at peace.

ATHEISM

Atheism is the belief that there is no god. A person who rejects the existence of god or gods is called an atheist.

AGNOSTICISM

Agnosticism is the belief that one cannot really know whether gods exist or not. Compared to atheists, agnostics do not outrightly reject the existence of God.

THE STORY OF SCRIPTURE

CREATION

Everything was created by God. He is the only uncreated being. He created the universe and everything in it. He created man in His image. He called His creation good (Genesis 1).

FALL

Adam and Eve, the first people created in God's image, disobeyed God, and sin entered the world (Genesis 3). The consequence of sin is separation from God and spiritual and physical death. The brokenness we see in our world today is the effect of sin.

REDEMPTION

From the beginning, God had a plan to save His people through the person and work of Jesus Christ, the Son of God. Jesus accomplished God's plan of redemption by putting on flesh, living a perfect life, dying on the cross to pay the penalty for our sins, and resurrecting three days later. He is now at the right hand of God.

RESTORATION / CONSUMMATION

The story is not over. At just the right time, Jesus will come again. This time, He will come as a judge, and He will make all things new. Not only will the penalty and power of sin be broken; when Jesus returns, the presence of sin will be no more, and He will dwell with His people again in the new heaven and new earth.

WHAT IS THE GOSPEL?

Jesus is the gospel. He is the good news. When Adam and Eve disobeyed God, sin entered the world, and sinful humans could no longer dwell with God who is holy. The consequence of sin is spiritual and physical death. The effects of sins are seen all around us in pain and suffering, death, natural disasters, and brokenness. But God had a plan of redemption from the very beginning. He would send His Son, Jesus, to live the perfect, sinless life we could not live. He would die on the cross to pay the penalty for our sins, and then He would overcome death and resurrect three days later. Now, He is at the right hand of God the Father. By His grace, God draws His people to Himself. We are saved by grace through faith in Christ alone.

Key Terms

JUSTIFICATION: *Justification is God declaring sinners not guilty.*

SANCTIFICATION: *Sanctification is becoming more and more like Jesus through the power of the Spirit.*

GLORIFICATION: *Glorification is the end goal of every believer. Believers will be free from the presence of sin and will eternally be conformed perfectly in Christ's image.*

Japan

Sea of Japan

MOUNT FUJI

MT. FUJI • TOKYO
• OSAKA

North Pacific Ocean

Philippines Sea

HIMEJI CASTLE, OSAKA

FAST FACTS

Continent - Asia
Area - 45,900 square miles
Population - 126,394,000
Capital - Tokyo
Main Language - Japanese
Main Religion - Buddhism (68.1%)

Freedom of Religion - Yes
Literacy Rate - 99%
Number of People Groups - 36
Number of People Groups Unreached - 23 (63.9%)
Population in Unreached - 123,749,000 (97.9%)
% of Professing Christians - 2.2%
% of Evangelicals - 0.57%

Kon'nichiwa! (Hello!)

My name is Takumi, and I live in Itabashi City, which is a special ward of Tokyo, the capital of Japan. Tokyo is a jungle made of buildings. Even at night, the streets are lit up and buzzing with people. Did you know that Japan is known for its use of robots? Technology is a big deal here. My dad is a professor at Teikyo University, a campus not too far from our apartment building. My mom stays at home to take care of me and my little sister.

One day, my dad led a trip for his students to serve the homeless people in a park in downtown Tokyo. When he was there, he became friends with a man who worked a lot with the homeless men in that park. His new friend was actually a missionary from the International Mission Board, and over time, he told my dad about Jesus. Suddenly, everything changed! My dad was more joyful, and our family started talking and laughing more. Then my dad took us to church, and we met other people who believed in Jesus. Many of them came alone; it is rare for whole families to be Christians here. Our family is the only one in our church.

My friends started asking questions about my family when my parents pulled me and my younger sister, Yuna, out of our after-school prep classes. In Japan, all kids go to extra classes after school. Even kids in elementary school go to classes at night because there is a lot of pressure for them to protect their family's reputation. They don't want to fail their exams. But after my mom put her faith in Jesus, my parents knew that they didn't need to worry about what other people thought. They wanted to teach us to look to Jesus for our worth and not academic success.

I didn't really know what to think at first. Like my friends, I thought Christianity was just for people with blue eyes – you know, a religion for people in Europe and America! Plus, even though people in Japan are free to choose any religion, most people don't identify with organized religion. Before Christianity, my parents were the same way. They didn't follow the religion of their parents. My paternal grandparents were Shintoist, so they worshiped the emperor, the sun, and other idols. My maternal grandparents were Buddhist, which is the most popular religion in Japan. My parents just worked hard and tried to be good people.

Since our family started following Jesus, we have experienced less stress and more joy. I have really enjoyed spending more time with my dad as he helps me study for my exams. My sister and I have been able to play outside together more. Our neighbors have noticed the positive changes, and they are curious. Our family prays every day that they would know God's love for them. We pray that they would not see Christianity as a foreign religion or something that goes against their culture and heritage. I pray for my friends at school because they are stressed and unhappy. I am very grateful that we have a church, even though it's small. Please pray for us!

Your friend and brother in Christ,

Takumi

PRAYER REQUESTS

Pray that the Japanese people would reject the popular belief that Christianity is only a westernized religion. Pray that the Japanese people would understand that God loves them.

Pray that the overworked and stressed people in Japan (young and old) would find comfort, worth, and true rest in Christ.

Almost 500 towns or villages in Japan do not have a church. Over 50% of the people groups are unreached. Pray for open doors and willing servants of Christ to go and proclaim the gospel.

DISCUSSION QUESTIONS

Less than 1% of Japan's population are followers of Christ, and over 123 million Japanese are unreached. How does that differ from where you live?

There is freedom of religion in Japan, but most Japanese people do not identify with organized religion. Why do you think that is?

Why do you think Japanese people think Christianity is a western religion?

North Korea

YANBIAN

China

TUMEN RIVER

THE KUMSUSAN PALACE OF THE SUN

Sea of Japan

★ PYONGYANG

Korea Bay

South Korea

FAST FACTS

Continent - Asia
Area - 46,540 square miles
Population - 25,654,000
Capital - Pyongyang
Main Language - Korean
Main Religion - Non-Religious (Atheism)

Freedom of Religion - No
Literacy Rate - 99%
Number of People Groups - 5
Number of People Groups Unreached - 2 (40%)
Population in Unreached - 25,466,000 (99.3%)
% of Professing Christians - 1.7%
% of Evangelicals - 1.57%

Annyeong-ha-seyo! (Hello!)

My name is Jane, and I live in Yanbian. It is a district within Jilin province in Northeast China. I enjoy living here even though China is not my home country. Last year, my mom and I crossed the Tumen River in the middle of the night. We were on a mission to get out of North Korea, which is where we are from. There is a lot of security between China and North Korea; there are even electric fences along the river. The journey was very dangerous and hard. We prayed that we would make it, and God protected us! There are actually many North Koreans hiding in China. Our prayer is that we will be able to make it safely to South Korea soon because it is dangerous to hide in China as North Koreans.

You may be wondering why we wanted to leave our country or why we couldn't just take an airplane. You see, North Korea is not like other countries. It isn't even like South Korea, the country that is directly connected to it. After World War II, the Korean peninsula separated into two countries: North Korea and South Korea. The division between the two counties is kept by a zone called the DMZ. It stretches across the entire peninsula, from sea to sea. That's about 150 miles! It's also between 2 and 3 miles wide. No one is allowed in the DMZ; in fact, for those who might try to cross, it's very likely they would die because they would be shot.

South Korea is a constitutional democracy like the United States and Great Britain. Its citizens have freedom and enjoy a lot of things like universal health care, advanced technology, and higher education. Unfortunately, that is not the case in my country. You see, North Korea is a socialist state. After the division, the Kim family took over. Kim Il-sung was the first leader, and he wanted everyone to worship him. He made a huge statue of himself in the capital and made everyone wear a badge with his picture on it.

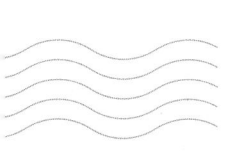

Today, his grandson, Kim Jong-un leads the country. Despite what is written, North Koreans experience very little freedom. Life is hard.

My dad was a farmer all of his life. He met my mom while working in a rice paddy. Just like his parents, my dad believed in Jesus. But my dad told me things were different when he was a little boy. Back then, there were many Christians in North Korea. There were so many that the capital was nicknamed the "Jerusalem of the East." But that all changed under Kim Il-sung's leadership. Because he wanted everyone to worship him, he destroyed church buildings. Today, there are a few official churches, but they are mainly for show. The leaders want the world to believe there's freedom of religion, but there isn't. Christians are severely persecuted. Even saying Jesus's name can cause you to join the tens of thousands of Christians in terrible labor camps. Here, worship has to be done in secret. My dad led one of the underground house churches. There would be a few adults gathered in a circle. I was always the only kid there. I had to be silent as I joined the adults in prayer and Bible reading. As I got older, my parents secretly taught me about the Bible. The good news they told me about was different than what I was learning in school, which was about the Kim dynasty.

One day, my dad was taken with no explanation. We knew it was because he was a Christian. My mom knew they could come and take us to a prison camp too, so we had to leave. Thankfully, my parents had a plan, and God protected us through it all. We never got to say goodbye to my dad, but we pray for him every single day. We pray that North Korea will be open to the gospel and that many will be saved. Please pray with us!

Your friend and sister in Christ,

Jane

PRAYER REQUESTS

Pray for the people in North Korea. Many children are starving and forced into labor. Many are also taught in school to worship the Kim family instead of God.

Pray for the more than 50,000 Christians in North Korea who are in detention centers and prison camps for their faith. Pray for their strength, protection, and release.

Pray that God would break the Kim family's regime. Pray that God would open North Korea to the gospel. Pray for the underground churches to remain strong in the meantime.

DISCUSSION QUESTIONS

North Korea is a unique country because it is a hermit kingdom. This means that the leaders of this country make it their goal to close off the country from the rest of the world. Why do you think they would want to do this? What negative impact would this have on the people of the country?

North Korea is often in the news for nuclear weapons. Sometimes, it's easy to forget the ordinary citizens of the country. What can you do to remember the people of North Korea who are often suffering?

People in North Korea can be put in prison camps just for saying, "Jesus." How does that differ from where you live? Does knowing about this country make you appreciate your country's religious freedom?

Turkey

HAGIA SOPHIA

Bulgaria
Black Sea
Greece
ISTANBUL
ANKARA
Georgia
Armenia
MT. ARARAT
Iran
Syria
Iraq
Mediterranean Sea

THE GREAT THEATRE AT EPHESUS

FAST FACTS

Continent - Asia
Area - 779,452
Population - 84,249,000
Capital - Ankara
Main Language - Turkish
Main Religion - Islam (96.2%)

Freedom of Religion - Yes/No
Literacy Rate - 96%
Number of People Groups - 68
Number of People Groups Unreached - 45 (66.2%)
Population in Unreached - 83,499,000 (99.1%)
% of Professing Christians - 0.6%
% of Evangelicals - 0.04%

Merhaba! (Hello!)

My name is Asya, and I am from Istanbul, Turkey. Istanbul is a unique city because it is transcontinental. This just means that half of the city is technically in Europe, and the other half is in Asia. You may have heard of Istanbul by another name in your history class: Constantinople! There is actually a lot of history in Turkey. In fact, there are historic areas in Istanbul that are on the United Nations' World Heritage List, and these areas are very popular with tourists.

Turkey is also the place where a lot of the Bible took place—there are more biblical sites in Turkey than in any other Middle Eastern country. Ever heard of Ephesus or Antioch? Those cities are in Turkey. You would think our country, which has been the backdrop of so much ancient Christian history, would be full of Christians. But sadly, that's not the case. Instead, less than 1% of people in Turkey believe in Jesus. As far as we know, we are the only Christian family in our district.

The way we heard the gospel was actually on satellite TV. One day, my sisters and I started watching a children's program that was broadcasted by SAT-7 Turk. My mom didn't mind because the show was educational and had a positive message. She actually started watching the different programs with us, and we realized the message of love and hope we were hearing was from the Bible. My mom started watching the shows for women and began learning about the Bible and teaching us what she learned. She even got a New Testament in the mail for free by answering an advertisement. We have felt a lot of joy since we put our faith in Jesus.

My dad has noticed the change in us, but we haven't told him about our new relationship with Jesus yet. You see, the main religion in Turkey is Islam, and my dad is a devout Muslim. In our country, faith and culture go together. There are a lot of expectations for my mom because she is a woman, and she is the wife of a Muslim man. My mom grew up with these expectations, but she didn't feel joy inside her heart. In fact, many Muslim women live in fear because their faith tells them that they may never really know God because of their gender. They are afraid because they never know if they're doing enough or if what they're doing is even right. There is a lot of shame simply because they are girls. So when my mom put her faith in Jesus and experienced joy and peace for the first time, she knew it was real. And she told us about the gospel of Jesus because she wanted us, girls growing up in a Muslim country, to know that we can confidently know Jesus and have joy and peace because He is enough for us.

It is hard being a Christian in a Muslim country. There are a few small Protestant churches in Istanbul, but it is too dangerous for us to attend right now. Please pray for Turkey. Pray that SAT-7 would continue to break down prejudices against Christianity and allow Muslims to hear the true gospel of Jesus Christ. Pray for protection against persecution and other unrest in our country.

Your friend and sister in Christ,

Asya

PRAYER REQUESTS

Pray for peace in the land amongst different ethnic groups.

Pray for open eyes and hearts; pray that Muslims in Turkey would have full revelation of the truth of the gospel of Jesus Christ and His Word.

Pray for protection and strength for persecuted Christians in Turkey. Pray for open doors for evangelism. Pray for growth in local churches.

DISCUSSION QUESTIONS

What do you think and feel when you think about Muslims? Do you see them as fellow image-bearers of God? Do you have any prejudices against them?

Back 1500 or more years ago, Turkey was a place of growth for the Christian faith. However, now the country suffers from misinformation about Christianity, and there is much resistance to Christianity. Why do you think that is?

The Muslim faith is tied closely to the culture in Turkey. What kind of unique challenges are there when culture is interconnected with faith?

Saudi Arabia

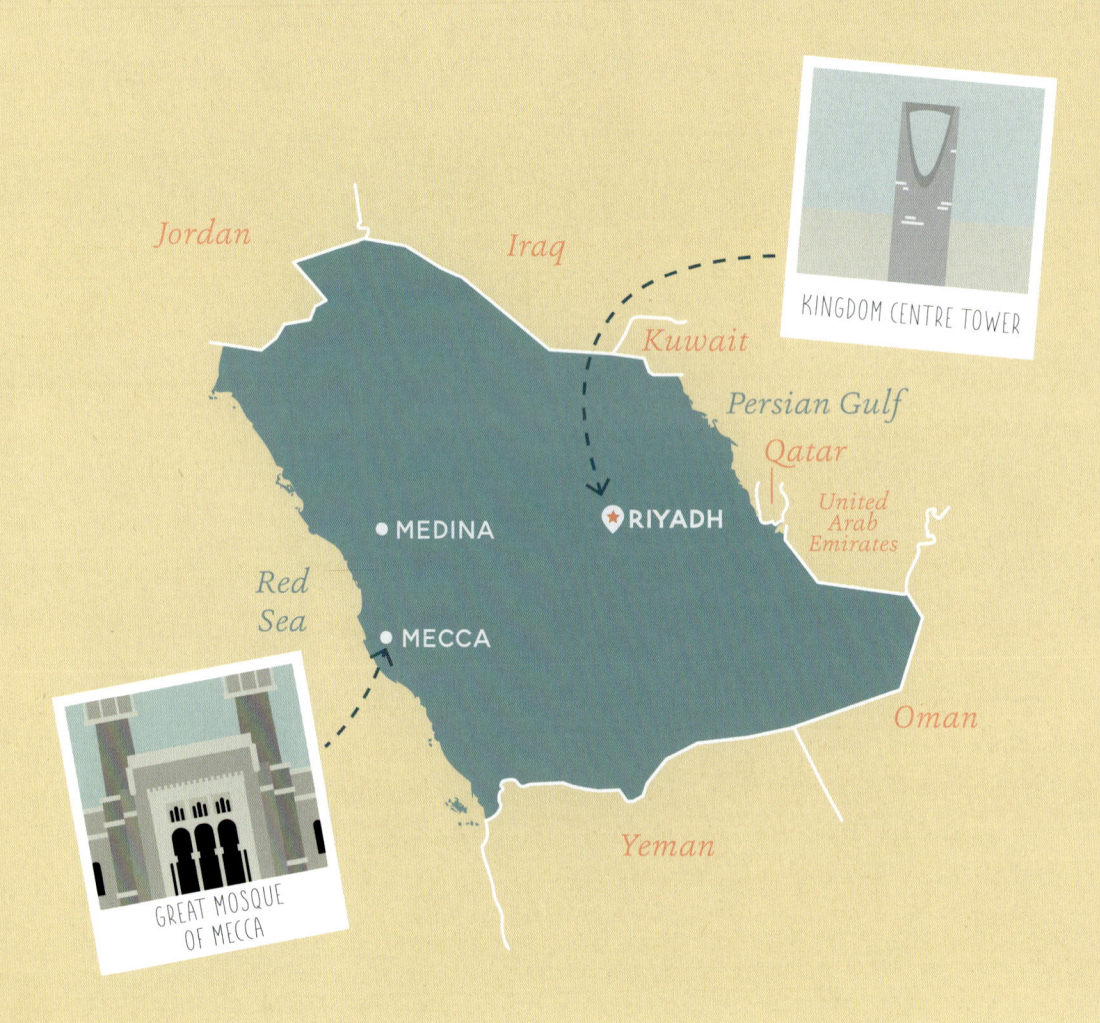

Jordan · Iraq · Kuwait · Persian Gulf · Qatar · United Arab Emirates · Oman · Yeman · Red Sea

MEDINA · RIYADH · MECCA

KINGDOM CENTRE TOWER

GREAT MOSQUE OF MECCA

FAST FACTS

Continent – Asia
Area – 830,000 square miles
Population – 34,737,000
Capital – Riyadh
Main Language – Arabic
Main Religion – Islam (91.8%)

Freedom of Religion – No
Literacy Rate – 95%
Number of People Groups – 44
Number of People Groups Unreached – 28 (63.6%)
Population in Unreached – 31,640,000 (91.1%)
% of Professing Christians – 4.3%
% of Evangelicals – 0.56%

Marhaban! (Hello!)

My name is Eva, and I live in Saudi Arabia, which is the largest nation in the Middle East. My family moved here from Great Britain when I was a baby because of my dad's job. Saudi Arabia is well known for its oil production. It is also the birthplace of the religion called Islam. Followers of Islam are called Muslims, and it is actually a law that all citizens of Saudi Arabia profess to be Muslims. This is because Saudi Arabia is a theocracy, which just means that there is no separation between the government and religion. In fact, the nation's laws are actually informed by the Quran which is Islam's religious text. Did you know that the two most important landmarks of the Islamic faith are in this country? You may have heard of them: Mecca and Medina. When Muslims all over the world bow down to pray every day, they turn to face the direction that points their heads toward these two places! One of the major pillars of the Islamic faith is a pilgrimage to Mecca! Millions of Muslims make this journey every single year.

Because we are British citizens and foreign workers in Saudi Arabia, we are not required to adhere to religious laws. We believe in Jesus. However, we do not have religious freedom. We are not allowed to worship outside of the privacy of our own home; there are no public churches anyway. We are also not allowed to wear cross necklaces or read the Bible in public. We respect the national laws, and we understand that businesses are run in accordance with Islamic laws. For example, Muslims pray five times daily — at dawn, noon, mid-afternoon, sunset, and evening. Businesses close in accordance with those times of prayer.

It is very difficult being a Christian in Saudi Arabia because public expressions of faith are not allowed. This means that we are not allowed to pray or worship in public. My family quietly worships in one of the bedrooms in our apartment. This can feel isolating, but we know that it is even more difficult and dangerous for Saudi citizens who are Christians. According to statistics, there are over one million—praise God! These citizens risk intense persecution and even death, which is the penalty for rejecting the Islamic faith. We have connected with some of these Christians over the years, mainly online. My dad regularly enters online chats in order to encourage these believers with the Bible.

Please pray for Saudi Arabia. God is working here, for a little over 100 years ago, there were only about fifty Christians. Pray for the safety of all believers!

Your friend and sister in Christ,

Eva

PRAYER REQUESTS

Pray that God would work to break down the strongholds of Islam.

Pray for the safety and protection of the 1.5 million Saudi Christians. The penalty for apostasy (rejection of Islam) can escalate to death. There is no religious freedom.

Pray for the people's basic human rights, and pray for the advancement of women.

DISCUSSION QUESTIONS

How does it make you feel to realize that there is a country in our world today requiring that its citizens profess a faith that is false?

Do you believe that God can pierce through the darkness of unbelief, even amongst the most devout Muslims?

Not all people are guaranteed basic human rights like freedom of speech and religion. Women in Saudi Arabia received the right to vote in 2015 and the right to drive in 2018. Crosses are prohibited, along with Bibles and non-Islamic religious gatherings. What can you do to advocate for these people?

Bangladesh

AHSAN MANZIL (THE PINK PALACE)

MYMENSINGH
SYLHET
DHAKA
India
Myanmar
Bay of Bengal

BAKLAI FALLS

FAST FACTS

Continent - Asia
Area - 55,980 square miles
Population - 163,945,000
Capital - Dhaka
Main Language - Bengali, English
Main Religion - Islam

Freedom of Religion - Yes
Literacy Rate - 58%
Number of People Groups - 331
Number of People Groups Unreached - 299 (90.3%)
Population in Unreached - 162,028,000 (98.8%)
% of Professing Christians - 0.3%
% of Evangelicals - Unknown

Assalamu Alaikum! (Hello!)

My name is Antu, and I am from Bangladesh. My country is small but full of beauty. It is next to India and near other countries like Myanmar, Bhutan, and Nepal. We have a long history—we were once part of India and then Pakistan, but we have been recognized as an independent nation since the early 1970s. It has not been easy though. You see, Bangladesh has the longest sea beach, and there are many rivers that run through the country too. Our unique tropical location means that we are susceptible to floods and other natural disasters. We even get hit with powerful tropical cyclones which are like hurricanes.

Bangladesh is crowded—there are lots of people living in a small space, even outside of the major cities. This can lead to challenges with public health, education, and employment, which all contribute to the lower literacy rate and higher poverty rate. I live in the Sylhet district in northeast Bangladesh. My parents run a tea garden. Our family is very blessed to have job stability, a secure home, and the resources to receive a good education. We are also grateful for religious freedom. As Christians, we are a minority in Bangladesh, which actually has a constitution claiming Islam as the official state religion. Most of the country's citizens are Muslim. There are also a lot of people who practice Hinduism.

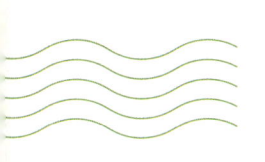

When we lived in Mymensingh, there were many more people who shared our ethnicity (Garo) and faith. We enjoyed gathering every week to worship. Although we will miss them, we find comfort in having the Bible translated into our language, and we have a heart for spreading the gospel to other ethnic groups in our country. There are over 100 million Bengalis in Bangladesh, and they are the largest unreached people group in the entire world. This ethnic group can be broken down into many smaller people groups, and they are scattered throughout Bangladesh. The majority of Bengalis in Bangladesh are Muslims, and we have seen that God is moving. There are many Muslims converting to Christianity, especially in the hill tribes in our area of Bangladesh. This has led to an increase in persecution for believers—many lose their jobs, and they are threatened and attacked for their faith. Some are even disowned by their families.

The cost is high, but many are seeing the beauty and truth of the gospel of Jesus and believing. Please pray that the gospel continues to spread. Pray for the protection of believers and the boldness to proclaim the truth, even if persecution and abandonment from their families are real possibilities.

Your friend and brother in Christ,

Antu

PRAYER REQUESTS

Pray for protection and provision for the people of Bangladesh who are often struck with natural disasters that worsen the already existing issue of poverty and illiteracy.

Pray that more believers would be willing to boldly proclaim the gospel and serve the Bangladeshi people, especially the Bengali Muslims (part of the largest unreached people group in the world).

Pray for protection and favor for Christian leaders in Bangladesh. Even though there is religious freedom, the state's official religion is Islam, and there is a great resistance against preaching the gospel to Muslims.

DISCUSSION QUESTIONS

Of the 162 million people in Bangladesh, 160 million are unreached. This means 160 million people may have never heard the gospel. How does it make you feel knowing that so many people in our world today have never heard the gospel and may not even know what the Bible is?

Extreme poverty and the lack of a good education are realities for many Bangladeshi people. Natural disasters can worsen the situation. How can the gospel give them hope when they are hurting physically, emotionally, or financially?

It is possible that Muslims who convert to Christianity can be disowned by their families and lose their jobs. The cost of following Jesus is high. Have you thought about the cost of following Jesus in your life?

Egypt

Mediterranean Sea

ALEXANDRIA •
★ CAIRO

THE GREAT SPHINX

Libya

NILE RIVER

Red Sea

PYRAMIDS OF GIZA

Sudan

FAST FACTS

Continent – Africa
Area – 390,121 square miles
Population – 102,256,000
Capital – Cairo
Main Language – Arabic
Main Religion – Islam (86.2%)

Freedom of Religion – Yes/No
Literacy Rate – 75%
Number of People Groups – 42
Number of People Groups Unreached – 25 (59.5%)
Population in Unreached – 12,445,000 (12.2%)
% of Professing Christians – 13.1%
% of Evangelicals – 4.45%

Iz-za-ac! (How are you?)

My name is Masika, and I am from Egypt. It's funny that my name means "a girl who was born during the rain," because a large part of Egypt's land is the Sahara desert. Most citizens live near the Nile River because it is the main source of water. You have probably heard of Egypt. Maybe it was in a Bible story about Moses leading the Israelites out of Egypt. Or maybe it was in history class while learning about hieroglyphics, mummies, and pyramids in Ancient Egypt. Our country has a long, rich history because it dates back further than most countries!

Ever heard of a guy named Alexander the Great? He founded Alexandria which is now the second-largest city in our country. That is where I live with my mom, dad, and three sisters. It is near the Mediterranean Sea. This is also where it's said that Mark—the author of the gospel of Mark in the Bible—planted the church that is now known as the Church of Alexandria. As a family, we are members of the Coptic Orthodox Church, which is part of the Church of Alexandria. Copts make up the largest Christian community in the country. But it's still a small number compared to the total population, which makes sense because the official state religion of Egypt is Islam. The majority of our friends and neighbors are Muslim Egyptians. This is because Egypt was invaded by Arab Muslims in AD 642. But the Coptic Church was strong and has now survived more than 2,000 years.

The history of my family and the Coptic Church reminds me to be strong in my faith. Christians in Egypt are often persecuted today. Many Christians have left Egypt because of religious tension and a lack of safety. Egypt has some degree of religious freedom—followers of Islam, Christianity, and Judaism are technically protected by the government to practice their religion and have public places of worship (like church). But that doesn't always stop people from looking down on and trying to hurt people in the religious minority (non-Muslims). A few years ago, there was a bombing in our city at Saint Mark's Cathedral. Many Coptic Christians died. A few years before that, there were a series of burnings of properties that belonged to Christians. There are many other stories of persecution, and it can be scary at times. But my dad always reminds us to trust in God and take our fears to Him in prayer. Instead of moving us to a safer country, my parents are teaching us to be bold in our faith.

Even though my sisters and I sometimes find the rituals at church to be strict, we see the joy and love that my parents have because of their faith in Jesus. Christians are strongly discouraged from sharing the gospel with Muslims, but my parents never hide their faith. They share the gospel whenever they can because they know the biggest thing our friends and neighbors need is Jesus Christ. Please pray with us that many more Egyptians will come to saving faith, and please pray for our protection!

Your friend and sister in Christ,

Masika

PRAYER REQUESTS

Pray that God would work to break down the strongholds of Islam.

Pray for true religious freedom for all people that is equally and thoroughly safeguarded by the government.

Pray for the protection of Christians in Egypt who are persecuted. Pray for boldness and favor for believers to share the gospel to the unreached in their own country.

DISCUSSION QUESTIONS

Egypt is in many Bible stories—from Moses and Pharaoh, to Mary and Joseph. The gospel even spread to Egypt after Pentecost in Acts 2. But now, Islam is the official religion with over 85% of Egyptians identifying as Muslim. A Christian nation doesn't always stay that way. What is the religious status of your country?

Many Christian Egyptians are leaving Egypt because it is dangerous due to increased persecution. What if your family had to move away because it was dangerous to believe in Jesus? How would that change the way you viewed your faith?

Even though Arab Muslims invaded Egypt in AD 642 and forced many Christians to become Muslims, there was still a group of Christians who remained faithful. God is able to sustain His people. How does that encourage you in your faith?

Morocco

Strait of Gibralter → *Mediterranean Sea*

HASAN II MOSQUE

Atlantic Ocean

RABAT
CASABLANCA

Algeria

SAHARA DESERT

Western Sahara

FAST FACTS

Continent – Africa
Area – 274,460 square miles
Population – 36,819,000
Capital – Rabat
Main Language – Arabic, Berber
Main Religion – Islam

Freedom of Religion – Yes/No
Literacy Rate – 69%
Number of People Groups – 31
Number of People Groups Unreached – 27 (87.1%)
Population in Unreached – 36,805,000 (100%)
% of Professing Christians – 0.2%
% of Evangelicals – 0.1%

Ahlan! (Hello! Welcome!)

My name is Amsah, and I am from Casablanca, Morocco. Morocco is a small country in northwestern Africa. It is actually very close to Europe. The Strait of Gibraltar, which connects the Atlantic Ocean to the Mediterranean Sea, separates the two continents. The narrowest part of the Strait is only 8.9 miles wide. This is why Morocco looks very close to Spain on a map. Casablanca is a bit further down the coast of the Atlantic ocean. It is actually the largest city in Morocco and a huge tourist attraction.

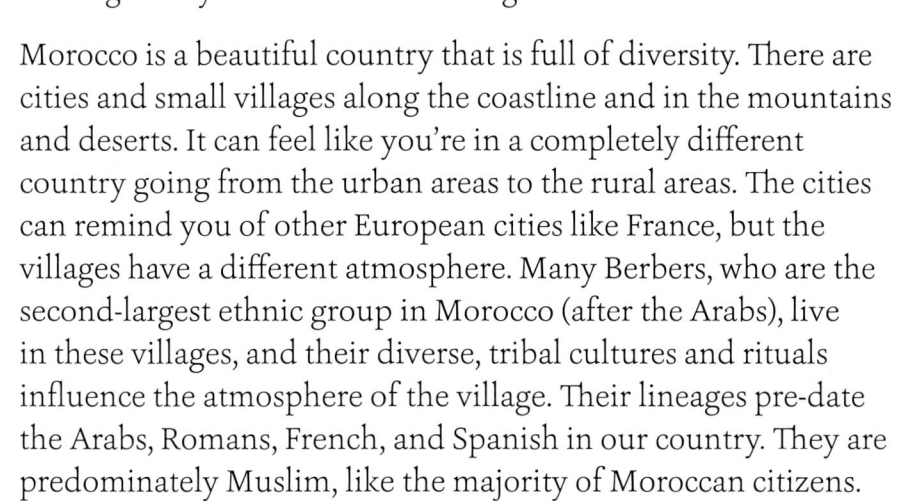

Morocco is a beautiful country that is full of diversity. There are cities and small villages along the coastline and in the mountains and deserts. It can feel like you're in a completely different country going from the urban areas to the rural areas. The cities can remind you of other European cities like France, but the villages have a different atmosphere. Many Berbers, who are the second-largest ethnic group in Morocco (after the Arabs), live in these villages, and their diverse, tribal cultures and rituals influence the atmosphere of the village. Their lineages pre-date the Arabs, Romans, French, and Spanish in our country. They are predominately Muslim, like the majority of Moroccan citizens.

There is a deeply rooted history of Islam in our country. Morocco has a king, and he calls himself the Commander of the Faithful, acting as a protector for the Islamic faith. This is why there are many rules. No one is allowed to publicly criticize Islam; if you try to witness to a Muslim so that he or she will convert, you could be heavily fined and put in jail for two years. There is also the possibility that you can be deemed a threat to public order and kicked out of the country. The government also makes sure everyone's television broadcasts the Islamic call to prayer five times a day. A certain percentage of the total broadcasts are also devoted to Islamic religious content as well.

There is technically religious freedom, but many Christians have experienced prejudice and persecution. Our family meets with two other families every week in our home. Even though there are officially recognized Christian churches that we can attend, my father wants us to stay under the radar of government surveillance so that we can better share the gospel with others. It's hard to be a secret worshiper, but I know it's necessary.

The way we heard about Jesus was from missionaries that were our neighbors. They were from America, and they were caring for a few abandoned children in the streets of Casablanca. This made my father ask questions. After a few months, we realized that they were working with a Christian organization. They were believers of Jesus who fully respected Moroccan laws. They were inviting these children to live with them in order to give them warm meals, clean clothes, and the chance to go to school. They were loving them, not trying to convert them. But one day, the police came, took the children, and told our friends they had only a couple of hours to pack up and leave Morocco. We were all shocked!

They showed us the love of Christ, but their story also showed us the great cost of following Jesus in a Muslim country. Please pray for the thousands of secret worshipers in Morocco.

Your friend and brother in Christ,

Amsah

PRAYER REQUESTS

Pray for ways the Bible and other evangelistic resources can reach the many unreached people groups in Morocco.

Pray for the Islamic government to ensure religious freedom. Pray that the unwarranted monitoring and prejudice against the religious minority would be broken by the power of the gospel.

Pray for the believers in Morocco who often worship in secret due to the issue of government surveillance and social persecution. Pray for protection and the ability to fellowship together in order to encourage one another.

DISCUSSION QUESTIONS

Just because the government claims to offer religious freedom doesn't mean that they actually protect religious freedom. Many Christians were forced to leave Morocco because of their faith. How would your view of Christianity change if you were forced to move to a different country just because of your faith?

In Morocco, Islamic beliefs are taught in the school curriculum and on television programs. This encourages resistance toward Christians. How would you feel if someone didn't like you just because you believed in Jesus?

Berbers are native to North Africa, and there is great diversity amongst its different tribes. Many reside in villages with no wi-fi or other modern conveniences. How do you think the good news of Jesus will reach so many different people?

Mongolia

Russia

ERDENE ZUU MONASTERY

ULAANBAATAR

Altai Mountains

GOBI DESERT

China

ALTAI MOUNTAINS

FAST FACTS

Continent - Asia
Area - 604,250 square miles
Population - 3,218,000
Capital - Ulaanbaatar
Main Language - Mongolian
Main Religion - Buddhism (41.2%)

Freedom of Religion - Yes
Literacy Rate - 97%
Number of People Groups - 28
Number of People Groups Unreached - 22 (78.6%)
Population in Unreached - 3,156,000 (98.1%)
% of Professing Christians - 1.8%
% of Evangelicals - 0.87%

Sain uu! (Hello!)

My name is Temulun, and I am a sixteen-year-old boy from Mongolia. Mongolia is sandwiched between Russia (to the north) and China (to the south). I live right outside the capital city, Ulaanbaatar. Did you know that Ulaanbaatar is known as the coldest capital in the world? It can get down to -40°F in the winter! Between the high altitude and continental climate (which just means our weather is unique because our country is landlocked and far from any large body of water), we get hot summers and really, really cold winters. We used to live in the countryside in a ger, which is a big, round, one-room tent. My mom was the lead herder for our family because my dad worked in the city, which was a ten-hour bus ride away. I loved that life. We would move around as the seasons changed so that our animals could eat and survive. We would be able to take down our ger and load it onto a camel in just a couple of hours! This nomadic lifestyle has distinguished Mongols for thousands of years. My great-great-great-great-grandparents were known to move more than twenty times every year to tend to their herds of sheep, goats, yaks, camels, and horses!

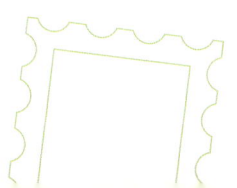

But one year, millions of animals died. Many herders had to move their gers closer to the city for work, and these neighborhoods became known as ger districts. We had to move, too. My dad chose a ger district by the hills outside of the city. During this time, my mom became very depressed. She was sad because the nomadic life was all she ever knew. She loved moving around our beautiful country and caring for the animals even though it was hard work. We were all worried about her. But one day, my mom started listening to a radio station. It was a Christian radio station, and she would listen to the people talk about family values and Bible stories. She started going to outreach programs while we were in school. We could see she was changing — she had joy and peace, and she told us it was because of Jesus!

We were amazed! Like most Mongols, we really didn't know about God or salvation. Growing up in the country, the people around us either practiced Buddhism or Shamanism. Then when we moved to the city, we realized that many people didn't believe in anything because that's what was taught when Mongolia was under the control of the Soviet Union. Almost 95% of Mongols fall into those three categories. Up until this point, our family had never heard of Christianity and the gospel of Jesus Christ. But once my mom got connected to a local church through one of the radio's outreach programs, she has been teaching us all about the Bible! My dad has even been open to learning because he has seen the change in my mom. While there may not be many Christians in Mongolia, there are churches that are growing and spreading the gospel.

Even though it was hard when we had to give up our nomadic lifestyle and move to the city, we can see how God was working. I am grateful to go to church and learn more about God through Bible study. I am grateful that I can go to school and learn new skills. One day, I pray that God will use me to spread the gospel to people all over Mongolia. There are millions of Mongols who have still never heard the gospel!

Your friend and brother in Christ,

Temulun

PRAYER REQUESTS

Pray for the training up and sending out of Christian Mongols to share the gospel with their people. The unique culture and harsh climate make it difficult for foreign missionaries to be as effective in ministry.

Pray for freedom from Buddhism and Shamanism, which are deeply rooted in the Mongolian culture. Pray also for freedom from atheism which is a product of previous communist rule.

Pray for unity amongst the Church in Mongolia and for favor as they reach out to the community to help people combat strongholds such as alcoholism and violence and offer them the good news of Jesus Christ.

DISCUSSION QUESTIONS

Did you know that about thirty years ago (1989), it was said that there were only 4 Christians in Mongolia? Now, there are over 40,000! Are there people in your life who you think will never receive the gospel? Take time to pray for them now.

Sadly, 98% of the population in Mongolia is still unreached. There are unique barriers in the country, including climate and culture. In what ways could these barriers be overcome? Do you believe God is able to overcome these barriers?

Mongolia is another country that is being positively affected by technology. Christian radio broadcasts are reaching people in the city and in rural areas where the nomadic lifestyle is still prevalent. What are the different ways we could share the gospel with others?

Afghanistan

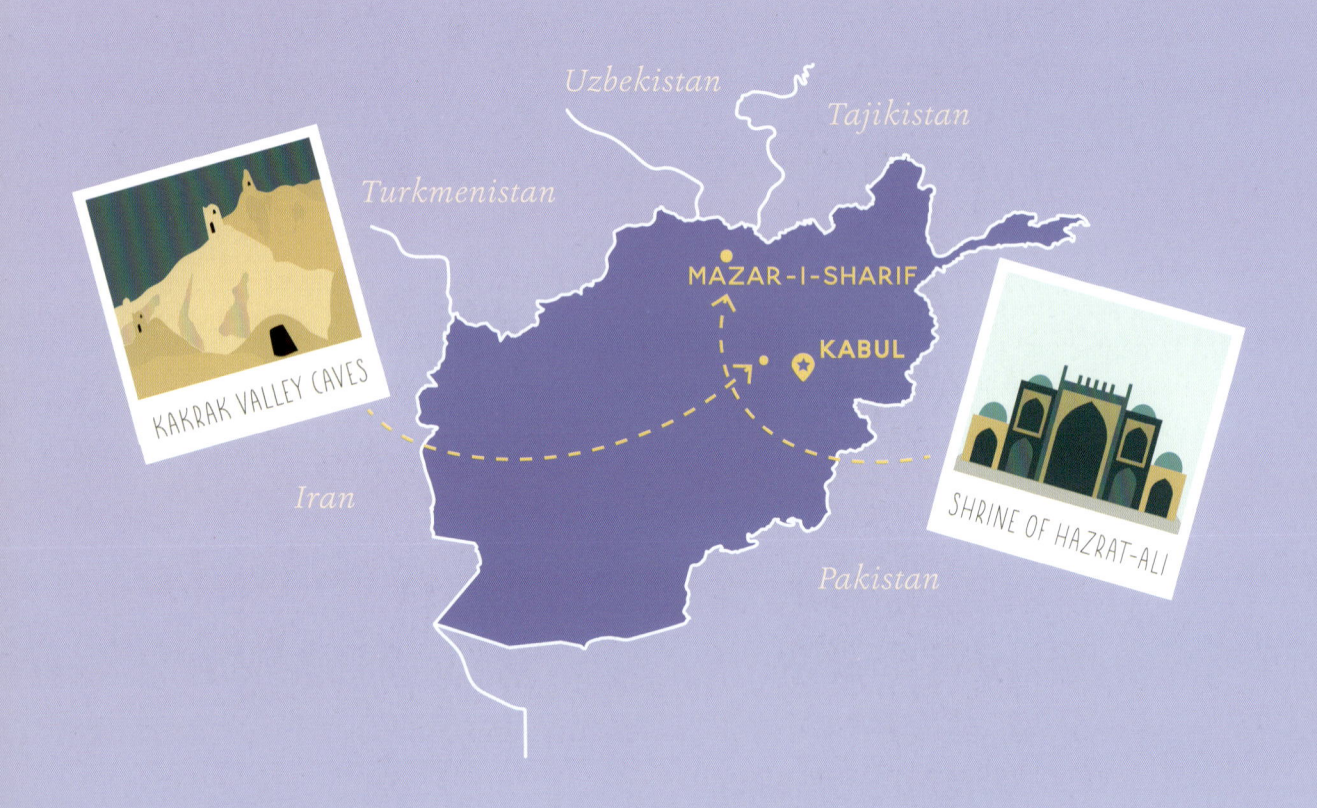

Turkmenistan
Uzbekistan
Tajikistan
Iran
Pakistan

KAKRAK VALLEY CAVES

MAZAR-I-SHARIF
KABUL

SHRINE OF HAZRAT-ALI

FAST FACTS

Continent - Asia
Area - 251,800 square miles
Population - 38,740,000
Capital - Kabul
Main Language - Dari, Pashto
Main Religion - Islam (99.8%)

Freedom of Religion - No
Literacy Rate - 32%
Number of People Groups - 72
Number of People Groups Unreached - 67 (93.1%)
Population in Unreached - 38,732,000 (100%)
% of Professing Christians - 0.1%
% of Evangelicals - 0.02%

Salam! (Hello!)

My name is Sahar, and I live in Afghanistan. What words come to your mind when you hear "Afghanistan"? Words like "war" or "terrorism" may come to mind. These are hard words, and sadly, they are realities for citizens of Afghanistan. You see, war has always been a part of my life. War has been a big part of my parents' lives, too. Most people only think about September 11th, 2001, and the war on terror after the World Trade Center tragedy. But the people of Afghanistan have been struggling with war long before that — with other countries and amongst our own people.

All of this war has really affected the normal, everyday citizens of our country. I think about my mom. When she was born in 1970, people were only expected to live to be 36 years old! She grew up in a poor family in a rural village, and she didn't have access to clean water. She didn't get to go to school to learn how to read and write, and instead, she married my dad when she was thirteen years old. This was normal for girls; instead of going to school, they married young. Thankfully, my dad was a tender man, and he treated my mom with love and respect. A few years after their marriage, they moved to the city because my dad wanted to keep my mom and two older siblings safe from the war between the Taliban and the government. My four sisters and I were born in the city, and Kabul has been our home ever since.

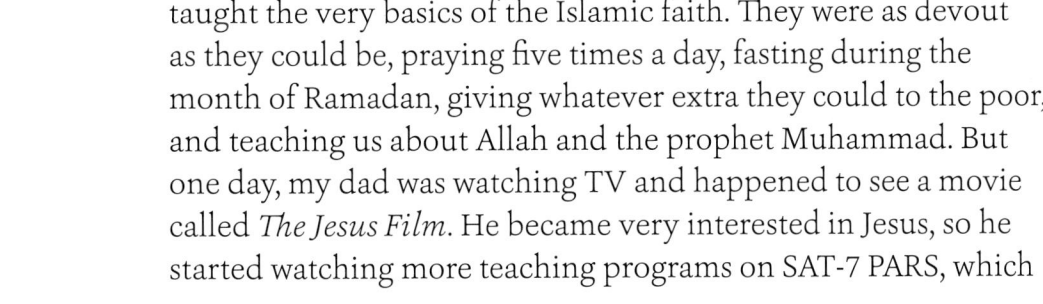

Both of my parents grew up in Muslim homes. They were only taught the very basics of the Islamic faith. They were as devout as they could be, praying five times a day, fasting during the month of Ramadan, giving whatever extra they could to the poor, and teaching us about Allah and the prophet Muhammad. But one day, my dad was watching TV and happened to see a movie called *The Jesus Film*. He became very interested in Jesus, so he started watching more teaching programs on SAT-7 PARS, which is satellite broadcasting. All of this was done quietly in our home because conversion to Christianity is considered a crime in our country. He had to be very careful. But we could tell that he was a changed man because of Jesus. He was always caring, but now he had peace and joy. He told us he felt loved and free for the first time, and he started teaching us about Jesus instead of Allah.

Our family worships alone in secret. There are no church buildings in Afghanistan. Converting to Christianity is like treason and is seen as a betrayal of country and family. There is a lot of persecution. My dad found the Bible online in our language, and we are memorizing it because we are afraid to be seen with it. We have heard of other families believing in Jesus and forming underground churches, and we are praying to be connected to a community soon. Please pray for the Christians in Afghanistan and for the spread of the gospel in our country!

Your friend and sister in Christ,

Sahar

PRAYER REQUESTS

Pray for social and political peace in Afghanistan. This country has been affected by war for decades, and there is a lot of suffering. Pray for the gospel to transform lives and usher in peace.

Pray that God would work to break down the strongholds of Islam.

Pray for the protection, strength, and encouragement of Afghan believers in the face of extreme persecution. Many have to worship in secret and lack access to biblical instruction and Christian fellowship.

DISCUSSION QUESTIONS

What words come to your mind when you hear, "Afghanistan"? Does your heart break for the suffering and injustice affecting Afghans? What can you do to see them as fellow image-bearers of God?

Converting to Christianity is a crime and seen as a betrayal of family and country. The stakes are high, and persecution is real. How would your view of faith and fellowship with other believers change if you didn't have the freedom of religion?

Almost 38 million people are considered unreached in Afghanistan. Is it hard for you to believe that so many people have never even heard the gospel? If so, why do you think that is?

United Kingdom

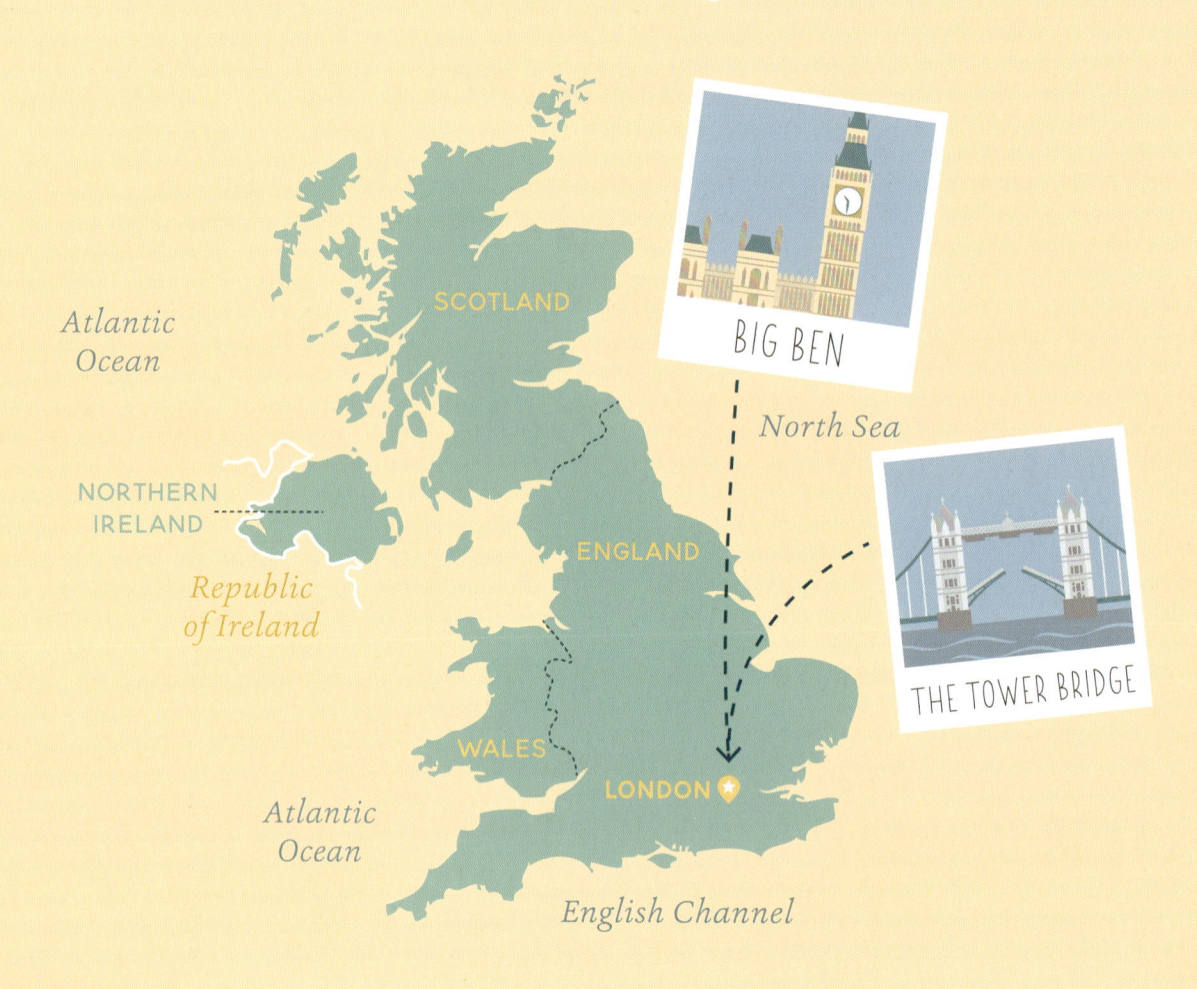

Atlantic Ocean

SCOTLAND

NORTHERN IRELAND

Republic of Ireland

ENGLAND

North Sea

BIG BEN

THE TOWER BRIDGE

WALES

Atlantic Ocean

LONDON

English Channel

FAST FACTS

Continent – Europe
Area – 98,628 square miles
Population – 67,839,000
Capital – London
Main Language – English
Main Religion – Christianity (57%)

Freedom of Religion – Yes
Literacy Rate – 99%
Number of People Groups – 113
Number of People Groups Unreached – 33 (29.2%)
Population in Unreached – 5,134,000 (7.6%)
% of Professing Christians – 57%
% of Evangelicals – 7.9%

Hello!

My name is Leah, and I live in London, England, which is the capital of the United Kingdom. Did you know that the U.K. is actually made up of four countries? England, Scotland, Wales, and Northern Ireland. London is the most well-known because it is the largest city in the U.K. and the home of Queen Elizabeth II. London is also known for famous landmarks like Big Ben, Buckingham Palace, the Tower Bridge, and the London Eye. It is a really cool place to grow up!

We live in Sutton, which is a borough in South London. My dad works with computers, and my mum is a nurse at the local hospital. My little brother and I go to school and tend to after school activities like most kids. When we're done, we usually play outside with our neighbors. They are from the United States, and they have five kids in their family! Last year, they invited our family over for dinner, and we got to know them. They told my parents about Jesus, and before we knew it, we were going over to their house every week for dinner and Bible Study.

London has all different kinds of people. There are over 300 languages spoken here — more than any other city in the world! There are people of all different cultures. My best mate is Korean, and we have friends in school who are South African, Indian, Pakistani, Chinese, and Caribbean. London truly is a global city. This diversity is seen in religion too. My friends are Jewish, Muslim, Protestant, Catholic, Mormon, and agnostic.

Before meeting our neighbors, we were agnostic. This just means we believed that people really couldn't be sure if God existed or not. My dad never really thought about it deeply. He honestly didn't care if there was a higher being or not. My mum, on the other hand, was always a bit more curious, but she's been so busy working and raising us that she hasn't had time to search. They both grew up in agnostic homes, and religion was never really a big deal.

But our neighbors shared the gospel with us, and for the first time, my parents realized that faith is a big deal! Since we have been going to this Bible study, my dad has been reading the Bible to us every morning. We are learning that knowing the gospel of Jesus Christ is a life or death matter. Now, I want all of my friends to know Jesus. It has been hard talking to my mates at school about it because they all think their religion is right. My prayer is that I would love them with the love of Jesus, just like our neighbors did and continue to do for my family. Please pray for us!

Your friend and sister in Christ,

Leah

PRAYER REQUESTS

The United Kingdom has a deep spiritual history. Its official religion is Protestant Christianity, but the church is in decline. Pray for revival and for a renewed desire for truth that is only found in the gospel of Jesus Christ.

London is a global city. Pray for believers in the U.K. to see the world right in front of them and step up to play their role in fulfilling the Great Commission.

Pray for the next generation in the U.K. to encounter followers of Jesus who are willing to share the gospel with them and engage in discipleship relationships.

DISCUSSION QUESTIONS

Just because a country states Christianity as its official religion doesn't mean that the country is full of believers. Missionaries are just as needed in politically and financially thriving cities. How can you live like a missionary in a global city, like London?

It is reported that there is a 97% chance that a person in his or her 20s in the U.K. has never in life encountered a follower of Jesus. Do you tend to assume that everyone has heard the gospel? How does knowing this fact challenge your assumptions?

London is a diverse city. Is your city diverse? What role are you playing in fulfilling the Great Commission in your city?

Cambodia

Thailand

Laos

ANGKOR WAT

MEKONG RIVER

IRRAWADDY DOLPHINS, MEKONG RIVER

PHNOM PHEN

Vietnam

Gulf of Thailand

FAST FACTS

Continent – Asia
Area – 69,898 square miles
Population – 16,662,000
Capital – Phnom Penh
Main Language – Khmer, French
Main Religion – Buddhism (82.2%)

Freedom of Religion – Yes
Literacy Rate – 77%
Number of People Groups – 44
Number of People Groups Unreached – 19 (43.2%)
Population in Unreached – 15,982,000 (95.9%)
% of Professing Christians – 3.4%
% of Evangelicals – 2.05%

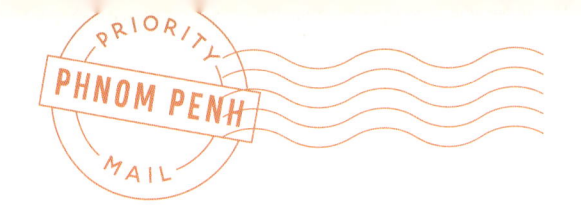

Susadei! (Hello!)

My name is Samnang, and I am from Cambodia! I am eleven years old, and I am the oldest of five kids in our family. We live in Phnom Penh which is the capital of Cambodia. Phnom Penh is a beautiful city, and we love living here with our parents. My family has lived here for generations. My dad tells us many stories about growing up in this city. One of the saddest stories is about the Khmer Rouge which was the communist party ruling our country in the 1970s. My dad was only five years old when they took control, but he remembers it well. Everyone was forced to leave Phnom Penh for years, and they were forced to work hard on farms. They were treated so badly that over 2 million people died.

My dad's parents were treated especially badly because they were Christians. They were tortured for just reading their Bible! By the time the Khmer Rouge was overthrown, there were barely any Christians left in Cambodia due to the intense persecution. Many were killed, and many fled to other countries as refugees. My grandparents survived, and my dad moved back to Phnom Penh with them when he was eight years old. It was a miracle! Seeing my grandparents stand firm in their faith in the face of persecution and death convinced my dad that the Bible really is true. He learned that following Jesus is worth it — even if it means death.

My dad works in a factory that makes parts for the Trans-Siberian Railway. This is a railway that's almost 6,000 miles long and runs across Russia. It is a famous train that many people still use today. We are grateful for his job because it provides for our family. Many Cambodians do not have good jobs. Poverty is a big problem here. My dream is to become a doctor one day so that I can give people money and free health care. It would be a wonderful way to share the gospel too!

The main religion in Cambodia is Buddhism. This religion has deep roots in our country, and almost everyone we know says they are Buddhists. Many of our neighbors are very interested in the supernatural world. There are many fortune tellers and people who say they can communicate with the spirit world. We pray that the Holy Spirit opens their eyes to see that Jesus is the only way, the truth, and the life! We go to a church in the city that was started by missionaries. We are so grateful for our church! Please pray that God will continue to add believers to our church so that we can work together to share the gospel and love the people of Cambodia with the love of Christ!

Your friend and brother in Christ,

Samnang

PRAYER REQUESTS

Pray that the light of the gospel would shine through the spiritual darkness in Cambodia.

Pray for churches in Cambodia. Ask God to strengthen and mature current believers to share the gospel and also tend to the community's physical needs.

Many children of Cambodia are forced into harmful work due to the extreme poverty in the land. Pray for their protection and deliverance.

DISCUSSION QUESTIONS

Cambodia endured a genocide. This is where a leader or group orders a large number of people to be killed. Many Christians were put to death because they believed in God. What if this happened where you live?

The Cambodian people have a lot of physical needs. Many live in extreme poverty. How could meeting someone's physical needs be a way to share the gospel?

Buddhism is the official religion of Cambodia. What do you think it would be like to be a Christian where Christianity wasn't the main religion? What hardships do you think you would encounter?

France

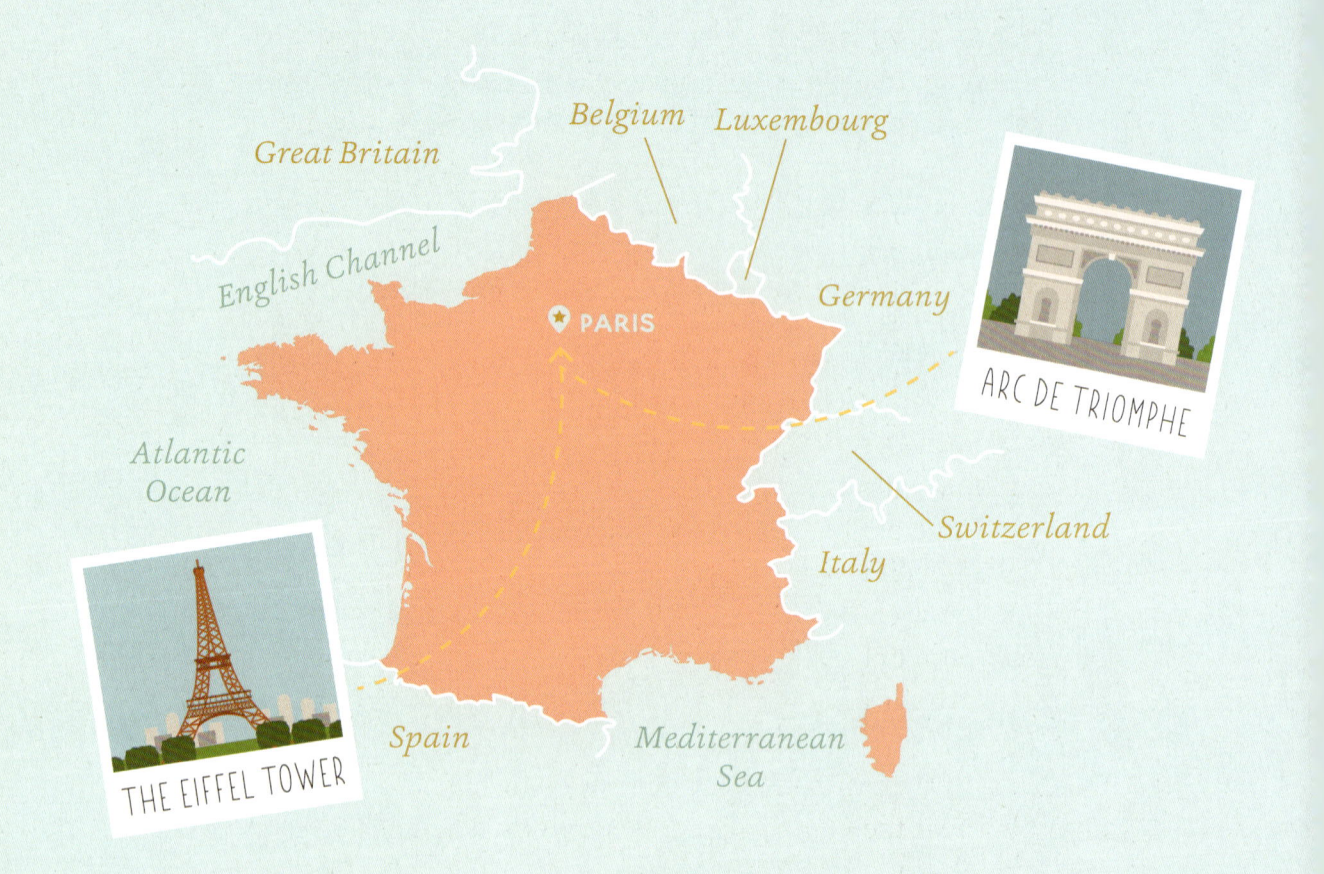

Great Britain
Belgium
Luxembourg
English Channel
PARIS
Germany
ARC DE TRIOMPHE
Atlantic Ocean
Switzerland
Italy
THE EIFFEL TOWER
Spain
Mediterranean Sea

FAST FACTS

Continent – Europe
Area – 248,573 square miles
Population – 65,064,000
Capital – Paris
Main Language – French
Main Religion – Christianity (62.3%)

Freedom of Religion – Yes
Literacy Rate – 99%
Number of People Groups – 113
Number of People Groups Unreached – 37 (32.7%)
Population in Unreached – 4,240,000 (6.5%)
% of Professing Christians – 62.3%
% of Evangelicals – 1.23%

Bonjour! (Hello!)

My name is Adele! I am sixteen years old, and I was born and raised in Paris, which is the capital of France. I live northwest of the city center in an area called Batignolles. I love Paris because it is rich in history and has beautiful architecture. The arts are really big here, too. There are a ton of museums and musicians, but the culinary and performing arts are also amazing! France is a very modern country and a big tourist destination. There are people visiting from all over the world, and many of them end up staying here! I love that my city is so diverse; I get to see people from all over the world become my neighbors!

When there are people from all over the world living in one place, it is common for there to be many different beliefs about God and religion. Some of my neighbors are Jews and practice Judaism, and others are Muslims and adhere to Islam. A lot of French people consider themselves to be Roman Catholic, but for many of them, religion doesn't play a big role in their lives. Interestingly, more and more people are openly saying that they are non-religious! They say that they are atheists, which means they don't believe God exists. Or they say they are agnostic, which means they can't be sure if there is a God or not. Honestly, when life is busy with school, work, entertainment, fashion, food, and friends, it is easy not to have much time to think about God and religion.

But for me and my family, religion is a big deal. We are one of the few families who are openly Christian in our area. I have found that it can feel very lonely being a Christian here. Many of my friends think Christianity is boring and old-fashioned, and sometimes, I feel like I don't fit in. My parents have even felt this in their workplaces. Many people don't understand why our family would choose not to enjoy some of the riches of Paris on the weekend and instead go to church and serve others.

Family is a big deal in France. We are very close. My older brother and sister are married and have their own families, but they live near us and always come over for dinner on Saturday evenings. My mother prepares a healthy meal for us to slowly eat together. It is also a time for our family to invite people over. It is unusual for French families to share these special weekend meals with strangers, but my parents use it as a way to share the gospel. Because family is such a big deal in our country, we have decided to share our most intimate family time to show others that they can be invited to the family of God. We have had so many different people gather around our table with us.

It was hard at first to share my family with other people every week, but I have seen how the love of Christ has changed people. It has changed me! Jesus is my hope and joy and peace. Even though I can feel lonely at times, I know I am not alone. Jesus is with me, and He has blessed me with my family. Please pray that our family and our small church in Paris would continue to be used to spread the gospel.

Your friend and sister in Christ,

Adele

PRAYER REQUESTS

Pray that the growing trend of secularism would break. Pray that the Holy Spirit would convict people of their sins and show their need for Him.

Pray that evangelical churches would continue to spread in France. Pray that those in France would not be suspicious of organized religion but that God would raise up believers who show the beauty of the gospel in their lives.

Pray that God would protect the young people of France who are struggling with despair and hopelessness. May they find refuge in the hope of Christ!

DISCUSSION QUESTIONS

France is a very modern country. Art, history, good food, and fashion are of great importance there. How could those good things distract people from their need for God?

It can feel very lonely being a Christian in France. Do you ever feel lonely as a follower of Christ where you live? How do you think that would impact your faith?

Many people in France say that they are Christians, but less than 10% go to church regularly. Why is it important for Christians to go to church?

Peru

Columbia
Ecuador
Amazon River
Brazil
MACHU PICCHU
Pacific Ocean
LIMA
BALLESTAS ISLANDS
Bolivia
BALLESTAS ISLANDS
Chile

FAST FACTS

Continent - South America
Area - 496,200 square miles
Population - 32,903,000
Capital - Lima
Main Language - Spanish
Main Religion - Christianity (94.1%)

Freedom of Religion - Yes
Literacy Rate - 94%
Number of People Groups - 104
Number of People Groups Unreached - 15 (14.4%)
Population in Unreached - 209,000 (0.6%)
% of Professing Christians - 94.1%
% of Evangelicals - 14.41%

Hola! (Hello!)

My name is Betsy, and I am nine years old. My family lives by the Amazon River in northern Peru. We are part of the Kokomas people, and we are one of the many indigenous people in the country of Peru. My mom, dad, and seven brothers and sisters live in a village called "9 de Octubre." Like most other Kokomas people, my dad is a fisherman, and my mom works on a small farm. My siblings and I attend the village school. It is a one-room schoolhouse, which means we all learn together. After school, we like to go to the library. This is very new to us. We have never had anything like this, but missionaries from America started this library, and they fill it with wonderful books, games, and toys! Sometimes, they even have people travel from Peru's capital city, Lima, to host fun weekends where they dress up as clowns and put on puppet shows.

Because my siblings and I have gone every day, we got to know these missionaries. Soon, my parents became curious about them. At first, they were very cautious. You see, these missionaries believe in Jesus, and my parents knew that their religion went against the traditional Kokoma beliefs. But they realized that my brothers and sisters and I were learning a lot, getting along, and becoming more joyful. We were being changed by the love of Christ that flowed through these missionaries. They would tell us Bible stories and share the gospel with us. Soon, we wanted to follow Jesus too, which made my parents really worried.

At first, they made us stop going to the library after school. But one day, my mom got a really bad toothache. She couldn't even go to work for over a week. My dad took her to the shaman who is respected as the village healer, but he couldn't do anything to help. My mom was getting sicker and sicker. Then my older brother told my dad about a man at the library who is a dentist. My dad didn't want to take my mom there, but she really needed help. The dentist was kind, and he quickly helped my mom feel better. Because she had to go see him a few more times, my parents started talking to the other people working at the library. By God's grace, my parents realized that there was something different about these people. They had joy, hope, and peace that was very uncommon amongst our village people. They were generous and kind, too!

Soon, my dad started studying the Bible with one of the men there. It wasn't long before he told my mom that Jesus was the one true God. Even though my mom was a bit hesitant to turn away from her belief in spirits and superstitions, she followed my dad and started studying the Bible. We started talking about the Bible more at home too. Our neighbors noticed the change in our family, but they were not open to turning away from the traditional ethnic religion. We are praying that God will work through our family to spread the good news of Jesus in our village!

Please pray for the few pastors and ministries near our village. There are not too many, but we believe that God can still do mighty work!

Your friend and sister in Christ,

Betsy

PRAYER REQUESTS

Pray for Peru's political and social climate. Peru's history is marked by war, corruption, and drugs. Over 50% of the population lives in poverty. Pray for just government leaders.

Pray that God would raise up Bible-believing people to serve the many indigenous people in Peru. Pray that God would break down walls between foreigners and natives. Pray that these missionaries would be rooted in the Word of God, and pray that the truths of Scripture will overcome the superstitions of various ethnic religions.

Pray that the Bible would be translated into the different tribal languages in Peru!

DISCUSSION QUESTIONS

Many people in Peru live in isolated villages, and they have never met people from outside of their villages. What do you think life would be like to live in a small village?

There are some villages in Peru that don't have the Bible in their own language. How does that change the way you view the Bible?

Some missionaries have shared the gospel with the people of Peru by providing medical or dental care or by helping them get clean water through building wells. What skills do you have that could help others and also be a way to share the gospel?

Russia

ST. BASIL CATHEDRAL

Arctic Ocean

MOSCOW

Kazakhstan   Mongolia   China   Pacific Ocean

MT. ELBRUS

FAST FACTS

Continent - Europe and Asia
Area - 6.602 million square miles
Population - 144,668,000
Capital - Moscow
Main Language - Russian
Main Religion - Christianity (57.6%)

Freedom of Religion - Yes/No
Literacy Rate - 100%
Number of People Groups - 185
Number of People Groups Unreached - 118 (63.8%)
Population in Unreached - 17,357,000 (12%)
% of Professing Christians - 57.6%
% of Evangelicals - 1.46%

Здороваться (Hello!)

My name is Demitri, and I am fifteen years old. I live in Russia, which is the biggest country in the entire world! It is called a transcontinental country which means that the country spans two continents—Europe and Asia. I live in the capital of Russia, which is called Moscow. More people live in Moscow than any other city in Europe! I live in an apartment with my mom, dad, and baba (grandmother). I have an older brother, but he is ten years older than me and already lives on his own. Most of the time, it is just me and my baba, so we are very close.

My baba takes me to church. I started going with her because of the brave stories of faith she told me about her dad. My great-grandfather was a Christian in Russia when it was very difficult to be. Back then, Russia was known as the USSR, which stands for the Union of Soviet Socialist Republics. It was a communist country, which means people didn't really own anything. Instead, the government owned everything, and everyone was supposed to share everything. It may sound nice on paper, but it was a hard time for people. There was a lot of oppression. The government was in total control and made a lot of rules. For example, the government closed churches, and Bibles weren't allowed. The secret police would often hurt pastors and throw them in prison. But my great-grandfather didn't back down from his faith. He believed in Jesus, and no one could change his mind. After communism fell, so many people said that they didn't believe in God. So many people didn't know the Bible, so my great-grandfather would teach whoever would listen!

Hearing about his faith lit a fire in me. I wanted to know more about Jesus, so my baba has been teaching me about the Bible. Now, Russia is more open to religion. It isn't perfect. The government still has a big say. For example, they give the most support to the Russian Orthodox Church, which is more of an institution than a church. There is also a law restricting the work of Christian missionaries. This law also makes house churches illegal. People are supposed to only go to churches that are on the list approved by the government. We are grateful to have a church to attend that believes in the Bible in Moscow!

Please pray for Russia. It is a big country with all different kinds of people living in all different kinds of climates. Lots of people struggle with poverty and hopelessness. There are many people groups across Russia who have never heard of Jesus! They are called frontier people groups, which means less than 0.1% of the population are Christians. This means that they need people outside of their villages to come and share the gospel with them. Many of the villages are secluded and deeply rooted in other religions like Islam or ethnic religions. Please pray that God would raise up Bible-believing followers of Jesus to share the love of Christ with these people groups. I pray that God uses me in that way one day!

Your friend and brother in Christ,

Demitri

PRAYER REQUESTS

Pray for true religious freedom in Russia. The government has been enforcing laws that have made it hard for Bible-believing followers of Jesus to minister in Russia.

Pray for the many Frontier People Groups (FRGs) across Russia. Pray that God would raise up believers to plant churches in these areas where the gospel has yet to be proclaimed.

Pray for the young people of Russia. There are many orphans, and nearly 1 million children live in the streets.

DISCUSSION QUESTIONS

There are many people across Russia who have never heard the gospel. Many of them live in villages where they need people from outside their villages to come and share the Bible with them. How would you feel if you lived most of your life never hearing about Jesus?

The government in Russia is strict about which churches people can attend. How does this change the way you view your church? Do you see your local church as a gift?

The persecution of Christians is a reality in Russia. What can you do today to strengthen your faith in Jesus? Even though you may not experience hard persecution where you live, you should hide God's Word in your heart so that you will always be prepared!

Indonesia

RAJA AMPAT

MT. BROMO

Malaysia

SUMATRA

JAKARTA

Pacific Ocean

Papua New Guinea

Indian Ocean

FAST FACTS

Continent - Asia
Area - 735,400 square miles
Population - 272,174,000
Capital - Jakarta
Main Language - Indonesian
Main Religion - Islam (82.1%)

Freedom of Religion - Yes/No
Literacy Rate - 93%
Number of People Groups - 789
Number of People Groups Unreached - 236 (29.9%)
Population in Unreached - 169,700,00 (62.3%)
% of Professing Christians - 12.7%
% of Evangelicals - 3.19%

Halo! (Hello!)

My name is Budi, and I am thirteen years old. I live on one of the islands that make up Indonesia. Did you know that the country of Indonesia is made up of 17,500 different islands? It's true! More than half of these do not have anyone living on them, but they are still considered part of our country. You can imagine how hard it might be for a government to manage all of these different islands. Plus, there are so many different people groups living in Indonesia. In fact, the different people of Indonesia speak over 700 different languages. Another challenge is that all of the islands are in the middle of the Indian Ocean and the Pacific Ocean, so there are a lot of natural disasters. There have been many erupting volcanoes, earthquakes, and tsunamis that have really damaged our people and land.

I live on the large island of Sumatra in the province called Aceh. Aceh is well-known because it is autonomous, meaning it has permission from the national government to operate under its own laws. It is the first province to have the Sharia law, which is a law requiring how Isalamic people should live. You see, the people of Aceh are extremely devoted Muslims. Even though the main religion in Indonesia is Islam, the people of Aceh are particularly known to be devout and said to be the starting place of the spread of Islam to the rest of Indonesia. My family has also strictly followed the Islamic faith for generations.

However, when a tsunami hit the part of Aceh where we lived, my dad met with some people who came to help our community recover from the disaster. They helped rebuild my dad's fishing boat and our house. My dad was very moved by their generosity, and he was shocked when he heard that they were Christians. He knew there was something different about them. He would tell us that these men had a peace and joy that was unlike anything he had ever felt or seen! Because he was curious, he continued to quietly talk to these men and heard the gospel of Jesus Christ. By the grace and power of God alone, my dad accepted Jesus as His Savior!

He was very quiet about his conversion for a while because he knew the persecution would come. He knew the persecution would even be toward us, his children. He knew our teachers at school would treat us badly, and our friends would abandon us. He knew our extended family members would also disown us, and there would even be a chance that we would have to move to a different province. More and more, the Muslims in our area have been extreme—even burning down many churches! All of this scares me, but my dad tells me that we don't have to be afraid. As he has secretly been learning about the Bible from these men, he has been teaching me, and we believe that Jesus is trustworthy and that He is the only way, truth, and life.

But please pray for our protection. Pray that we would be able to find a church and safely be able to worship and grow in our knowledge of God and His Word. Pray for our country!

Your friend and brother in Christ,

Budi

PRAYER REQUESTS

Pray for the many areas in Indonesia that are resistant to the gospel. Pray that God's kingdom would break through the spiritual darkness and stronghold of Islam.

Pray for the protection of believers in Indonesia. Persecution is a reality in this country that has more Muslims than any other country in the world.

Pray for Bible-believing churches. Though Christianity is one of the approved six religions in Indonesia, there has been a rise in extremist behavior. This is in addition to the many laws that church planters have to abide by to even start building a church.

DISCUSSION QUESTIONS

Many people who believe in Jesus in Indonesia are abandoned by their families who believe in a different religion. What do you think it would be like to be the only person in your family to believe in Jesus?

Persecution is real and hard in different places around the world. Have you ever experienced persecution for being a Christian?

Many churches in Indonesia have been burned down by those who oppose Christianity. How would not being able to meet with other Christians at church impact your faith?

Thank You

for studying God's
Word with us!

CONNECT WITH US
@thedailygraceco   @dailygracepodcast

CONTACT US
info@thedailygraceco.com

SHARE
#thedailygraceco

VISIT US ONLINE
www.thedailygraceco.com

STUDY CONTRIBUTORS

Designer
KATIE LINSTRUM

Editor
ALLI TURNER

www.thedailygraceco.com

Unless otherwise noted, Scripture quotations have been taken from the Christian Standard Bible®, Copyright © 2017 by Holman Bible Publishers. Used by permission. Christian Standard Bible® and CSB® are federally registered trademarks of Holman Bible Publishers.

Designed in the United States of America and printed in China.

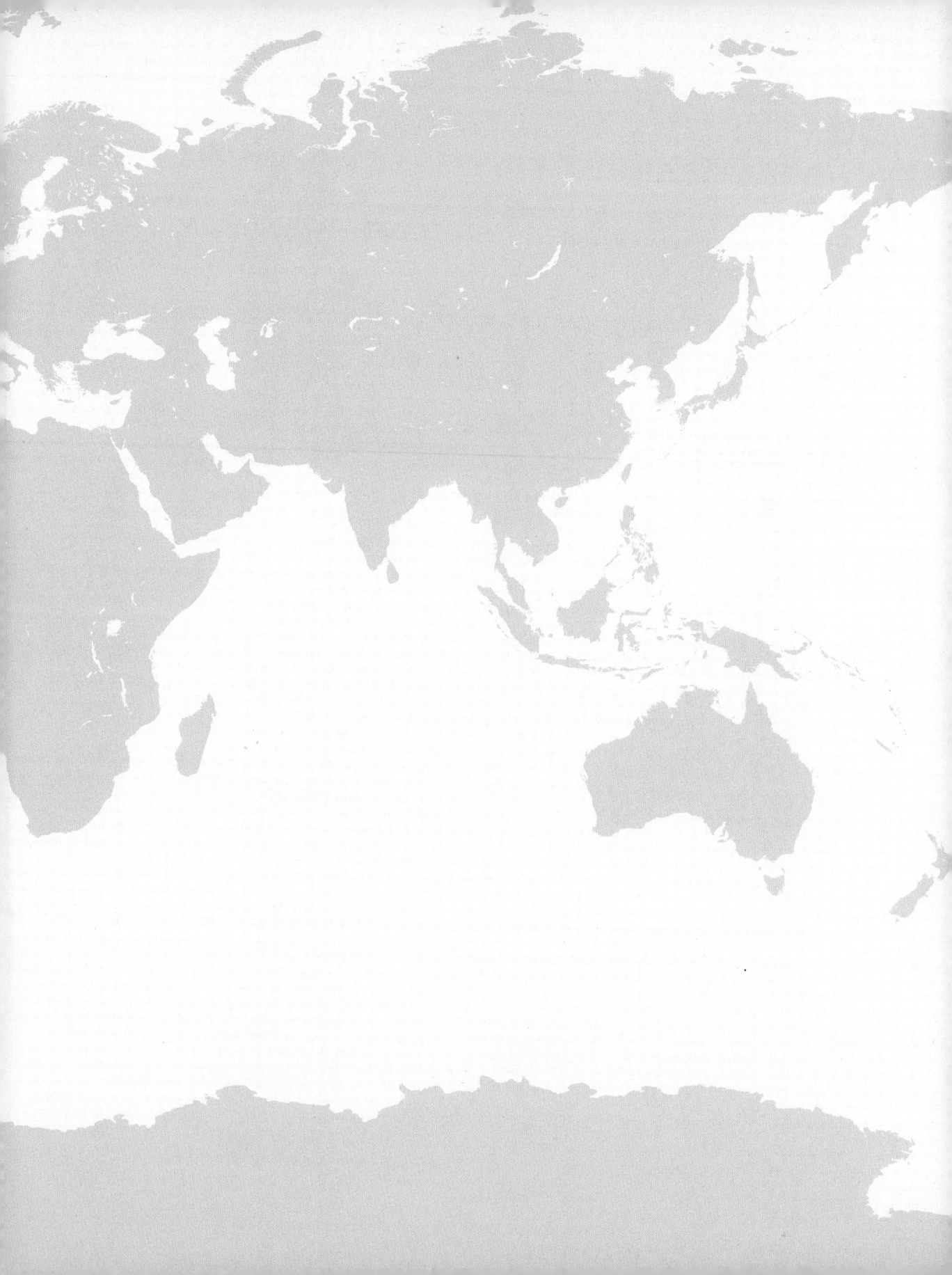

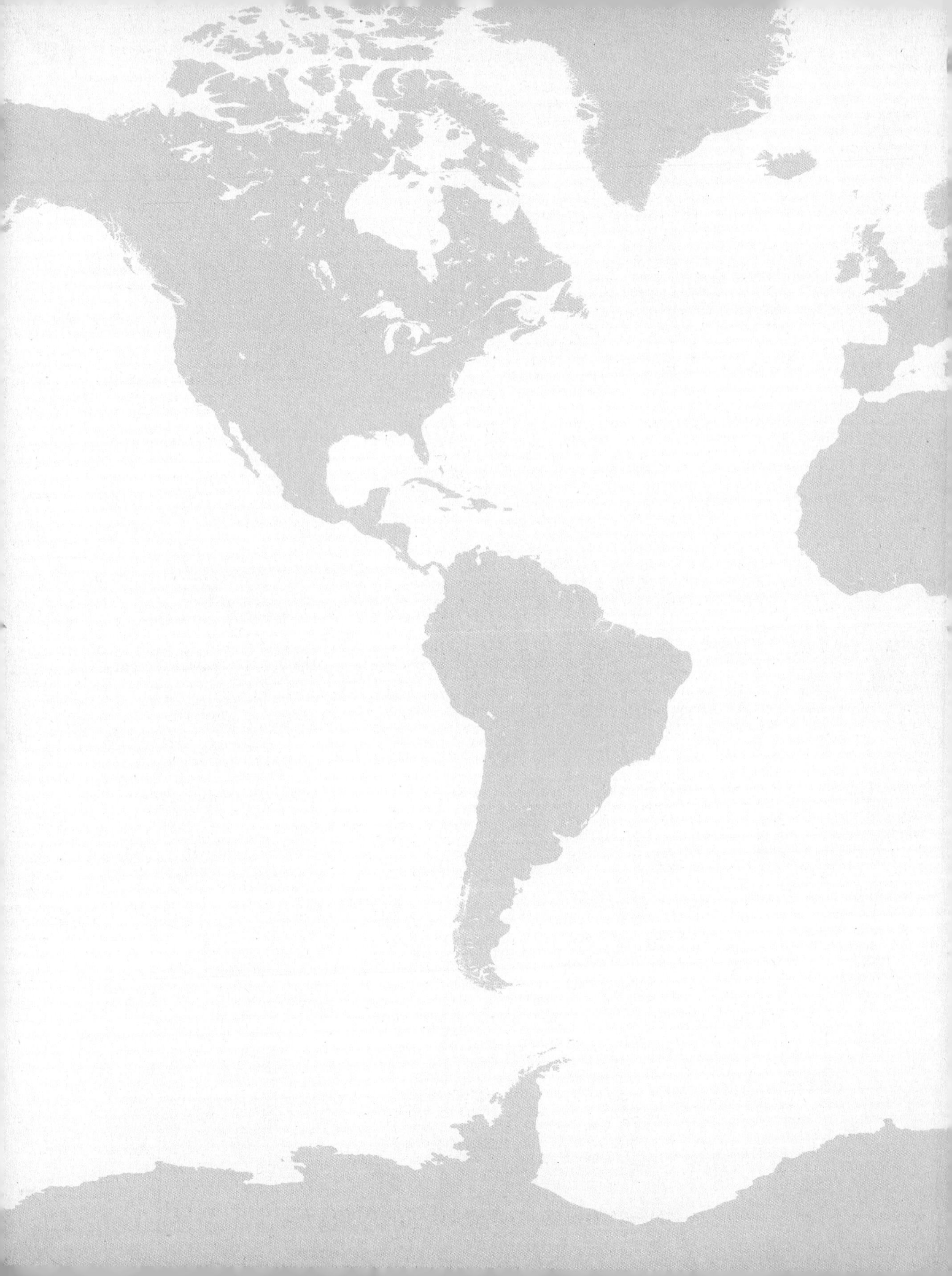